Amor Fati

To Love My Fate

Roderick Pittman

BookLeaf Publishing

India | USA | UK

Presentation by *BookLeaf Publishing*

Web: www.bookleafpub.com

E-mail: info@bookleafpub.com

ISBN: 9789358317220

First edition 2024

For Trae & Calvin.

You are remembered.

PREFACE

Twenty twenty-three sliced my soul in two. From spending time with my brother as he transitioned from this life, to navigating chaos in and around my home, I have questioned the purpose of my existence. I grew famished with a deep longing for Spiritual nourishment.

For a year I walked closely beside my brother Trae as he fought cancer. Distracted, I lost focus on the love that occupied my life which eventually ended in divorce. Unexpectedly, my young son moved in while the walls of my home were simultaneously crumbling down. I cut ties with some friends as I reevaluated familiar ties. I was also scratching the surface of a new career while grappling with the waves of change barging in from the world around me. My life had been filled with misunderstandings, mistakes and arguments, disillusions and pride.

Then my brother died.

Three weeks later my young cousin's life ended. Two intricate connections are forever gone as my emotions are provoked by voices I can't remember. All that's left are silent echoes.

The torrential rains of grief had knocked me completely off my feet while I was fighting to stand firm on the vision God had entrusted to me. To help curve some of the intrusive thoughts, I fell in love with reading again. I started reading books like *The Spontaneous Fulfillment of Desire* by Deepak Chopra; *You Are the Placebo* by Dr. Joe Dispenza; and *Outwitting the Devil* by Napoleon Hill.

While reading Susan Anderson's *The Journey from Abandonment to Healing*, I came across the phrase *Amor Fati* - a love of fate. The philosopher Friedrich Nietzsche describes it as "That one [who] wants nothing to be different, not forward, not backwards, not in all eternity. Not merely bear what is necessary, still less conceal it ... but love it." After one long night of partying, I went and had *Amor Fati* tatted on my chocolate brown skin with a double shot of bourbon in my left hand.

One month after my cousin's funeral, the weekend after I got my tattoo, 3 young men wielding guns threatened to kill me because of a misunderstanding. My light was nearly blown but that experience corrected my blurred sight. I lended myself to meditation to filter my subconscious mind while battling the negativity feigning for control. I began to focus on the life ahead of me. I was facing my fate.

As I surrendered to meditation, my dreams were resuscitated. Through the dark night, my soul was healed. I began to realize that restoration comes at a heavy price. Twenty twenty-three engendered psychosis of the heart but through the difficulties I've learned what it means to fall in love with my fate.

Most of the poems in this book were written as I managed the changes happening around me. Some may sound like a journal entry while others follow poetic styles such as terza rima, haiku, and sonnet. At the end of *Amor Fati*, I give insight on how I battled grief.

I hope that you find enlightenment, healing, and peace as my writings evoke reflective and meditative thought.

TABLE OF CONTENTS

Creation Story

Slow dance with me baby
Gentle whispers in my ear
Come closer darling, near'r
There's nothing for you to fear

We can tip-toe on morning dew drops
Slip and slide across the moon
Climb Eastern Pine and touch the tip-top
Lay underneath warm rays after noon

Slow dancing with me tender
Sweet whisperings graze my ear
Draw closer baby, near'r
I'll catch your lonely fears

I see your heartbeat in your stare
Rest easy I know it's new
Gripped tight, we're almost there
Bound together - sticky goo

Slow dancing, baby, tender
Whimpers sweep across my ear
Pull closer! Yes! Come near'r!
You need this, don't dare veer

Tapped fault lines then your earth quakes
Did I strike a nerve?
Rushing winds and our worlds shake!
Gushing waters beyond the verge

Swift dancing with me tender
Loud screams through deafened ears
Come closer draw me near'r
New life will soon appear.

Rushed Trip

Speeding down avenue "You"
Ignoring the bright red lights
Not taking in the scenic view
Rushing to get to our destination
Already there in my head so there's increased
anticipation
Slowed down…
Saw the cop coming from behind
Tapped the brakes praying I wasn't clocked this
time
No citation just a verbal warning
Out of view
Pedal to the metal
Let's keep on going
Sign says "Road Work Ahead"
"Detour around it" is what you said
Set back a few hours but that's ok
Drove through a storm going the alternative way
Fuel is low but no time to stop
Our destination's right around the block
The "Maintenance" light soon came on

Ignored it to enjoy our favorite song
A sudden gasp
Yet another delay
Caught in the tune
We went the wrong way
Our vacation trip a big disaster
Now we're sitting here stuck in Alaska
Cold.

Separated

5

Pensive thinking whirling bustling sigh
Your numb touches leave me disconsolate
We let distractions slow down our growth rate
Constant sparring blistered and marred our sight
Tasting lustfully sweet pungent delight
Blue lips tightly pinched, you grow petulant

Quiescent echoes, cold breath. You're reticent
One look would suffice - almond eyes,
brown-bright.
Lighthearted, you leave with full acceptance.
Two hearts bow out and carefully undress
a vision ridden and drenched in regret.
Punctuated but devoid a sentence
A noncommittal love we both professed-
Moonlit night, a ring, and a vapid bet.

If Love...

if love could shield heartbreak
    who would fall each time the same
are hearts that resilient
    to endure the weight of guilt, of shame
if love is the cure for heartache
    where comes the strength to mend
oh love why doest thou forsake!
    hell's fury you did awake!

let go of your pride
    i hold on to my ego
from love we can't hide
    it's a villain and a hero
subtract then divide
    miscalculated; this debt I owe

Emotions

Emotions can't be trusted
or be accepted on a whim
They are *intrusive* and **EXPLOSIVE!**
Brightened day or night dim

Like the wind that can't be seen
To and fro they swing and sway.
Ceaseless, TORRENTIAL RAINS.
Violent waves.
Death. Birth. Murderous pain.

Bi/polar & e-p-i-s-o-d-i-c
Thoughts **bursting** through the *silence*
DRIVING ME INSANE!
Piece-by-piece my peace mute and lame

Emotions can heal with zeal
Slow release of disdain
Forgiveness bound to hope provoking life
rearranged
New love is persuasive; not everyone's the same
Achievement, growth, and opportunities; access
to new terrains

Emotions can leave you incredulous
Uneasily trusted, helpful or vain

They can be *intrusive* or **EXPLOSIVE!**
Brightening sunshine or deadening pain.

Split Decision

Conflicted with who I am
This visage reappears
Choices. Decisions. What do I want?
Soul thirsting for happiness with no fear

Benign ponderings, stoic glance
I am my presence
Reflected through a tinted glass
Attracted and desirous

Two for one; a greedy quell
Shattered and broken - neither one can heal
Three lover's quarrel, a cunning deal
Commitment's not what you feel.

Toe-to-toe with conclusions
Consequences we can't elude
Either way the bet is lost
A spacious heart, an open field

Addiction

an abandoned child
Wandering with no place to go
Latching on to anyone's presence
Used and abused in each home

a defiant child
Adamantly not bossed around
Cajoling his host into passive acceptance
Manipulating emotions without a sound

a rambling child
Obsessively compulsive tauntings
rambling onward without rhyme
Intrusive solicitations, trespassing valuable time

a stubborn child
Persistent in folly's way
With no room for correction
Asked to flee but disobeys

Bottle of Sorrows

pop the cork
me sips
Alone
Except
bottles
hear me
a balm to
Salve my soul
Monkey riding my
back and back and back
A troublesome counselor
leading me to a seductive place of
Slumber with each pronouncement
drip'n over parched patches embedded
deep jagged holes. Inebriated on old
Stubborn ideas poured out like libations
offered up to a god unknown.
What proof I consider is but a
titter of comedic relief. Please
tell me the truth! Am I stuck in
cycles with where I whine o'er
what I cannot grip? Inside these
bottles are my life's sorrows. It's
a bevvied up version of falling
and standing on flimsy strands
of plans written on ol' papyrus
paper. Refracted glassy reflections of a
drearily long face etched between the
descriptive notes of this prescription I've
Become too attached to. Can I leave
behind all these vetted excuses? alcohol
was never useful. This red blood is black
against vintage dark green. Each sip
insidiously drains me. When I talk
with my bottle, I don't hear a thing.

Drifter

Abandoned and useless
Fighting battle after war
Standing tall with defeat
Weary. Tired. Worn.

Am I my own weapon?
Am I my enemy without a clue?
Do I avoid every lesson?
Cycling dirty residue

I want to trust Your timing
Learn Your voice and follow suit
It's You who made this decision
Sinful fool you chose to use

I am a lonely drifter
You're the wind against my sail
Where is it that You're leading
At best assured that I won't fail

Black Male Professional

Weak as a white elephant standing in the middle
of a room
Strength as silent as the dismay stuck in his
brow
Gait wobbly-crooked straight
Striking thunder with each tip-toe
across blood-stained concrete
Flat-footed swift pace
Slowly wandering through conquering defeat
Smells like the heat of battle
Aroma thick like the blood of stiff bodies hung
from trees
Seeking uncomfortable seats;
wounds opened and fresh
Swatting nagging gnats
and lies buzzing in his ears
Striving to find focus as he hears his ancestors
cheer

Rhythmic beat colliding with black skin
prancing through fires
Billows of charred smoke in late autumn, early
June

Weeping with every breath
Mourning turned to gloom
High expectations though they look down from
plastic moons
Overqualified and never justified.
Some young black boy's hero
Skin thick as silk
Cannabis cravings
Malted liver and liquored kidneys
Medication to sustain his drive
Vision cleared – taking hold of glory's objective
Pale obstacles and anger coincide
Weeding the garden of his mind
Black pride reflected
While wrestling to be professional

Uni-Verse-All

racial pride
superficial opulence
intellectual arrogance
religious bigotry
humanity's demise.

Lonely Seed

Reality is defined as what you actually perceive
But how many are blinded to all that is actually?
Consumed by their lies the blind cling to the
blind
Breeding a new nation of blind beginnings
That which now leads is that what we must now
defeat

Only those with sight can truly see
The Zeitgeist of present reality
We're hardly standing on our feet
Knees buckling under the pressure and the heat
Our true strength we must now seek

To be guided I can't be blinded
To move forward I can't run from it
Even without the credentials to save a nation
There is a nation still yet to be ruled

I once was blinded
But now I see
Amazed by grace
The roaring sea

Lord as I rise
Please humble me
You are my potter
I'm in Your knead

I am Your seed
Please flow through me
So others blind
My charge to lead

Remove the blinders!
You've parted seas!
Our past inside us
We fear we need

A tree is but
A lonely seed
Avoids the birds
Outsmarts the chipmunks and the squirrels
Survives and thrives to grow towards the Most
High

Trampled under many wars, battles, and defeats
Yet it outgrows the grass

And outlives the leaves
Stands tall and strong
While still yet being that lonely seed

Tao

19

Validation I avoid
Completion - my choice
Melting snow slips through my hands.

The Dichotomy of Fear and Freedom Pt. 2

Caught betwixt the dichotomy of fear and
freedom
The choice to love what I know is truth
I have to face this reflection erect in the mirror
No deceptive cloak or second-guessing proof
Why fight against what I truly are
A star is but a shining star
Conformity leads to destruction
With unrealistic hopes and faulty reconstruction
Tauntings and ridicule
Beams leaning on the walls of acceptance is a
foundation weak
Self-acceptance is my weapon
Righteousness in conscious individuality
Weird or strange; judge my name
Heavy rejection, sorrowful disdain
In a world full of criticism
Where they all strive to be the same

I'll embrace this struggle
I'll swim through the rain
This fight with adversity
My freedom to gain

The Burden of Freedom

Looking, striving, seeking perfection
Without avoiding reflection and self-correction
Is there a pure state of being?
Do I search until the end of me?

Compulsive obsessive over slow changes
Reassessing battles, victories, defeat
I can't walk sure blindly
Consequences tickling my feet

What is the profound meaning
Why do I find nothing but bleak?
I can't control everything
Blind acceptance and determination compete

Decisions to make constantly
Life is what I choose
The freedom to walk the path I seek
Or do nothing and choose to lose

Ordered and patrolled – patrolled and ordered
Someone else guiding me
With no sense to make of my own
Though being conscious is my destiny

So I correct my stance
With a peculiar glance
Whoever I am steps in front of me
Respectful chances
To live, walk and, dance with
this burden of being free

Sedated Confession

I couldn't recognize what love was growing
among thistle and thorn.
Spur-of-the-moment altercations between two
hearts I adore
Love unrequited; forced reconciliations and
momentary peace
Nothing pure and authentic
Love was difficult to meet.

Love was a hidden agenda.
Requested but I couldn't receive
I became a self-fulfilling prophecy sowing
suspicions, betrayal I'd reap.
We get what we project into this world; my
projections produced defeat
But my thirst for love drove me back up on my
feet.

Microscopic lenses fault finding in defense
Expecting lies led to misdealings; frequently I
repented
Manipulation was protection
Deception's a cloak to cover dirt.

Accusations drive people crazy.
Or draws what insecurity persuades

Trying to control another's actions will leave
you helpless and afraid.
100 thread count sheets on the beds I made

Suspicions became my existence
Poisoned by toxic interactions that left me
blinded and weak.
Anxiety highs and depressive lows.
In survival mode with an emptied soul.

I knew love, she was distrustful
I found her dangling off a ledge
Abandoned, doubled back for more chances
Heart shattered so she chose to flee

Love's a wingless bird
Dizzy, spinning, illusive form
Like a voice spoken off meter
Or fighting death though forlong

Little bro, love isn't that hard to find
My light is flickering but I see love all around
Medicated, I reflect on what was right and what
went wrong
You have more time, so live it bold.

Empty Frames

We shared few pictures
Wooden frames left void
Father & son, pride & joy.
Blank memories; soul sores.

Brick-by-brick stacked on diaphragm
Erected wall financed by tears
Heart beats it down with each vacant memory
How much I missed you, abandoned years.

Forgiveness is not the issue
Canceled debt, angry note
Too taxing to carry that burden
Though lies continue to provoke

Sigh.

I ponder ponds
Bedding bass, flat-headed catfish
Red wigglers and titty bream
Mischievous gators, sneaky snakes under limbs

Rusty boat rides on makeshift ships
Empty spaces for us to shore
Shared glimpses of an intimate life
Sunsets with clouds laced in gold

Old and worn and torn pictures
Wooden frames left void
Father & son, pride & joy
Blank memories; soul sores.

Afterthought

For lifetimes
I have been your
afterthought
It has solidified
It's wrapped around
a cage
with a key
that's been thrown
into the great
abyss.
And it's falling
And it can't be fetched.

Last Breaths

help me! help me! How can this be?
A draft reminiscent; but I can't breathe.
I'm mourning my existence; Je soif vie.

In the throes of death, drawn into a quandary
I wait on time left, what's next I can't conceive
help me! help me! How can this be?

Will this moment bring closure? Will I sail the
waves of eternal peace?
Muffled mummerings, borrowed strength - I
must release.
I'm mourning my existence; Je soif vie.

Arpeggio; broken chords, progressing
keys played in concert to a melodic dream.
help me! help me! How can this be?

The metronome of my plight is tuned to a tragic
scene.
Give thee all thine love now! I demand with
conceit!
I'm mourning my existence; Je soif vie.

As I painfully surrender to find abundant relief
Paralyzed and losing sound – refusing to so
easily leave
help me! help me! How can this be?
I'm mourning my existence; Je soif vie.

At Deathbed
(09/12/2023, 02:12pm EST)

I would have never left your side
Through the heartaches and raging tides
Your life was lived in musical strides
Knowing that God is your eternal Guide
Man judges from the outside
God sees deeper than you or I
Your heart broken, was made of gold
Loving with hesitation, an old and deep soul
We wrestled vigorously through our plight
Bumps and bruises awakened at night
Times were lonely and we were sad
But we knew what we had
Keep reaching for the light
I'm here by your side
It won't be long
Nonresponsive fading glow
You're already gone

Memories

What are memories?

Mental images trapped in mind
No one else can see them

They can be touched by no one
Only seen by the one close in sight

Memories appear real
So close, so distant
Rewound, and scene in new perspectives
Focused through blurred lenses

Memories hang in the balance of past and
present
With the doors to reality closed forever
Wild adventures passing by
Nothing more than abstract imperfections

What are memories?

Can they be erased?
Will they be replaced?
How can I escape…

Suicidal Memories

I still feel the throbbing on the right side of my
brain
Though it's not dilapidating
I feel like I've been elevated from the
underworld where demonic forces patrol
An aroma of lavender leaves and falling petals
from roses
I'm happier today and I'm sure my face glows
But I wish I could control those hazy days filled
with suicidal thoughts
When the world seems to have crashed and
everything's my fault
And my life halts to the silent screams
modulating inside of me

Orgasmic wishes for sunlight kisses
From the beautiful rays of a new day
When my mood sways in the wind of
nightmare's air
Broken wings
Fire blossoming trees
Stranded in the desert
Thirsting the waters from the drought-drained
Nile
A peasant searching for a morsel to comfort his
only surviving child
Patiently waiting the days of "after a while"

Forceful smiles through chapped lips
Uncertain steps
Lonely strolls to find an empty space to place a
chaise of happiness
The place that I'm near
But I fear depression's return
I've filed suit against it
Restraining order
Trespasses
And then arrested

I feel like I'm being molested by my past
I want free at last!
And not just these subtle victories
Not a mark left by a dog on a tree
Or a release of pressure through a mental valve
This throbbing on the right side of my brain
I feel insane expanding; growing pains
Pride wants me silent and in hiding
But my soul knows I'm losing control

I can't remember the days
As a keyless piano is played
And depression sways to the tune
At the reception of mental oppression and
doom's day

Suicidal Honeymoon!

I still feel the throbbing on the right side of my
brain
Though it's not dilapidating
I feel like I've been elevated from the
underworld where demonic forces patrol
An aroma of lavender leaves and falling petals
from roses
I'm happier today and I'm sure my face glows
But I wish I could control those hazy days filled
with suicidal thoughts
When the world seems to have crashed and
everything's my fault
And my life halts to the silent screams
modulating inside of me

*If you are someone you know is struggling
with suicidal thoughts, call 1-800-273-8255,
911, or 988. There's help for you.

Death

Lost in the routine and confusion of each day
Silent while patiently working its way
Dark.
Cold.
Lonely.
Misunderstood.
Death's a face we'll all meet
Some see it as defeat and grow afraid
Others claim it as victory, a gift for the journey
they've made
Many are unmoved, death's unknown
A complex surprise like a king dethroned
Overlooked yet never forgotten
A powerful force only conquerable by Christ
An unsolved mystery
A road mapped by those who can't guide
An unanswered question
A voice without sound
After death is there a place to reside?
Do the dead watch over loved ones after they've
received a crown?
Are they rewarded with wings so they can flutter
around?
With a world as cruel, who would want to be
reunited with this ground?
We live our lives with such guarantee

No one's promised another day to be
Neglectful moments we ignore to partake
Putting off today for tomorrow, oh what a big
mistake!
Living for pleasures forsaking purpose
One day to realize that death's always patiently
lurking

Encore

On a walk this morning
I found a lonely bench
With my head bowed
And knees slightly bent
Blades of grass sword fighting in the breeze
Body rocking heartache swinging to 88 keys
Eyes full of fading memories
Misguided expectations.
Failed hope.
Mournful defeat
A gentle whisper asked, 'Do you see what I see?'
I look up to find my angel watching over me
I miss you.

A State of Being
(Meant To Be)

Meditation breeds elevation.
Elaborate conversations between Spirit,
  subconscious, and soul.
Accelerating metaphysical manifestations.
Nothing in this world is worth its weight in
  gold.
Transcendental proclamations.
Transacting penance in exchange for the
  birth-right sold.
Omnipotent coherence with slight trepidation.
Being in a state that allows destiny to unfold.
Events forthcoming as I've been shown.

Peace Lily

Without a good-bye
Your form limp and decompressed
Has life departed?
Vacant breaths and empty words
A moment later, reborn.

My Brother in Memory

I remember him playing piano in his element
He was free being who he was meant to be
Will I leave memories as relevant?

The beauty of life is found in each moment, I
now see
Abruptly crashing into who you are
Eyes shut and tightly closed and all there is is he

Mon frère left his mark; his death, a life-sized
scar
He found his purpose and lived by design
Before he departed, he was already a star!

Conformity? You can surely dismiss.
Focus on the now, grow into bliss.

ABCs of Being Present

All you need is now and free.
Between the charge of past and future are
Circuits of never-ending energy.

Do you hear destiny's call?
Empowered by the gods of light,
Forsake whatever betides, whatever befalls.
Growth expounds o'er the dark night.

How much longer will you run amiss?
Invictus! Captain! Take charge of your flight!
Just above a wink...a breath...a kiss...
Karmic sentiments on the brink of crossing o'er
Lamentations from a soul longing bliss.

Master! Come sit on your throne!
No time. No place. No body. No thing.
Open space for your Spirit to roam!

Possibilities unlimited; pure consciousness your
shroud.
Quantum observer and potentials; Quantum
leaps and bounds!
Reality Isn't what you might be thinking
Surrender to Now and you'll be found.

Transcend delusional demise
Unleash the power within you
Veer those pesky limitations
We walk by faith and not by sight!

Xenial Host awaits, arms opened wide!
Yield to your Higher Purpose
Zen moments flowing by-and-by.

In this present moment.

The Valley of the Shadow of Life

Divine Intelligence guides my mind;
  I shall not deviate.
I take rest in abundant possibilities;
  Source leads me to opulent streams.
Infinite Intelligence breathes life into my
present: God leads me into the paths of
  freedom for His name's sake
Ye though I walk through the valley of life I will
be cautious of my decisions;
  for the benefits of time and hypnotic rhythm
are with me.
A resolute and definitive mind prepares a table
before me in the presence of
  harmony: Thou fills my head with wisdom; I
have more than enough to share.
Surely definiteness of purpose and definiteness
of plan will clothe me all the

days of my life: and I will dwell in the house of Mastery and
  Empowerment for ever.

A List of Dates

Spring ushered in my seed
   turbulent winds blew him into my arms
Summer burned my heart
   scorched the love out of my soul
Autumn revealed the true colors of a companion;
   old leaves don't live in new seasons
Somewhere in between I fell for an illusion
   accepting a lie, ignoring the truth
My brother labored to celebrate another year,
   ten days later he took flight back home
I called on Monday 3 weeks later
   by Thursday my cousin's life was gone
Gathered pieces from violent misunderstandings
   reconciled but still dethroned
Found coping in bars and bottles
   three black boys almost snuffed me out
Three days later dreamt of an old friend
   a year prior on the same day his life gone
Thankful to taste the daily bread of life I had
forsaken
   Wisdom and grace to accept the negligence of
my plans gone wrong

Cumulative Arrogance

Have you ever gazed into the blurred eyes of
puffed-up figurines unfurling in an air of
grandeur enshrouded upon themselves, escaping
the integrity found in humility's form?
With temerity, they move unfettered, aimless,
and blithe as they ubiquitously rise bold. Self-
proclaimed regal monarchs, surfing the wind
like clouds, placid and demure. They cast shade
on those below, exalted above what was
yesterday's home. Whether vain or with a brain
inundated with fog, they are benighted of the
looming monsoon. They undervalue being
grounded while prodigiously enrobed in
borrowed ivory cotton and outlined with
celestial gold hemmed with
distilled dross. Unconsciously pushed about;
mercilessly surrendering to abode's control.
These undulating clowns parade in exaltation
whilst cycles of precipitation dissolve their
throne.

Once the anticipation to grow pompous begins
to blow back in, remember that they will soon
again cleave to the fragmented sands of their
delicately evaporated ego.

Judged

Every man owns demons
Opened tab – they're pricey
Perplexing that we judge each other.

Goey, sticky labels
Shirt-pinned name tags
Have you placed your feet in their soles?

Misguided ramblings, painting portraits
though you'll never see the debris in their soul
Unconsciously judging another being

Are their thoughts on display?
Are they blown over a bullhorn?
Emotions sound familiar

What does anger say?
How can we ever judge another?
Yet it's something we all do.

If I judge you then you judge me
Who am I? Who are you?

Sleep Paralysis

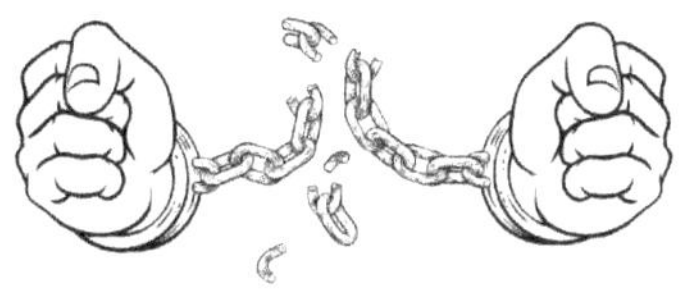

Worldly, roaming spirit
Awakened while in deep sleep
An aura sits softly at my feet
An invisible force hovered over me
Mysterious spirit suffocating; I can't breathe
Subtly stealing control from me
Thick cloud of electrons blinding
Body restrained
though that's not it's goal
Lips waxed shut
Arms heavy like cast iron
Legs nonexistent
Mind and soul whimpering,
"help me. help me."
Roaming spirit - unknown
Seducing defeat
Lame and mute
Tried to call out from a voice stolen
God's names escaped
No fear though I am weak
Feeble, cold, and harassed
This spirit, what did it seek?

Heavy pressure
Crushing depression
Chasing after destiny

SUDDENLY THE CURSE IS BROKEN!

Free at last!
Demonic forces flee.

Know Who You Are
(Affirmation)

The Most High resides inside of me.
I AM in the image of God.
I AM a physical manifestation of my Creator.
I AM One with God; I AM One with creation.
My mind is God's throne.
My body is God's temple.
God's presence agrees with me.

Note From The Author

Growing through Grief

Experiencing change throughout life can fill you with joy, such as the birth of your first child or graduating from college after working on your degree for years. But the somber side of change is when we are faced with loss such as divorce or the death of a loved one. Recalibrating after such detriment can become a confusing journey filled with uncertainty as you are forced to continue living life devoid of something or someone you once knew. Grief typically fills the void, but suffering through grief doesn't have to be a lifelong hindrance when reconsidering the 5 stages of grief from a perspective of growth. Grieving can become the catalyst that pushes you into a new life.

The first stage of grief is denial which is marred with delusions as you attempt to ignore the loss you have suffered. You may banter about how there's no way your boss could run the department without you, or you may pretend that your lost loved one will soon return from a long trip. The mind can be a tricky place when it doesn't know what to do with the feelings attached to what is no longer there. It's easy to deny it, but this pain you feel is what grief is all about.

No matter how difficult this stage may be, this could be the start of opening yourself up to the wonderful possibilities that lie ahead. As your mind attempts to persuade you that what you have lost is still relevant, you can use that same mental energy to imagine how you could be better if what you lost never left.

When my young cousin died 3 weeks after my brother passed away from colon cancer, I became numb. I imagined that he was still alive but too busy to return my missed call 3 days before he died. But eventually, I began to imagine the conversations we would have had if he were still here. We talked frequently about the power of meditation and finding life's purpose beyond the pain we both had experienced in life. Those imaginary talks led me to begin focusing on my future which led me to enroll in school and complete my degree.

Anger typically follows the denial stage. You lost your job, and you can't get over all the work that you'd contributed to support the company's mission. Your wife files for divorce after you've invested years into the marriage. You've watched a loved one slowly die of a disease that still has no cure, so you blame the doctors or God. Anger, which is a valid emotion, is the frustration of realizing that sometimes we have no control over the circumstances of life. Instead of moping around, caught up in a tizzy, you can redirect that energy into being productive by asking yourself questions that provoke growth.

What passions could you develop that you ignored for your career?

In what ways can you improve yourself for the love you may find in the future?

What gems of wisdom did your deceased loved one instill that if applied can make you a better person?

Don't avoid the anger about what has transpired but restructure your thinking and use that energy to heal and grow.

> *"Circumstance does not make the man; it reveals him to himself."*
> James Allen, As A Man Thinketh

Bargaining is a stage of grief that can be one of the most daunting and tedious phases. The what if's leave you stuck in a cycle of regret; however, this bargaining can be intrinsically beneficial for your growth. You may think that if you had done everything right initially, you may not have experienced loss. If you had only taken him to the doctor when he first told you his symptoms... If only you had not started your business then maybe you wouldn't be struggling financially... If only you had been a more nurturing parent, maybe your child wouldn't regard you with so much contempt.. The list can go on into infinity.

My brother told me about the symptoms he was experiencing before his cancer diagnosis. I insisted he visit a doctor sooner, but he convinced himself that he was alright. I never pushed the issue and then early one morning I received the call about his diagnosis. I was devastated and started blaming myself for not being more adamant with him about seeing a doctor earlier. There was absolutely nothing I could do about his condition, but I turned my bargaining into introspection and started being proactive about my own health.

I hadn't had a colonoscopy or any type of preventative examination in years. I couldn't force him to go to the doctor, but I could force myself. The bargaining stage can be a revelatory start for you to reason with yourself and be proactive prior to the vicissitudes of life forcing you to contemplate your own "if only" in retrospect.

"When we are no longer able to change a situation, we are challenged to change ourselves."
Viktor E. Frankl, Man's Search for Meaning

Grief is a lonely road that often leads to depression as you cope with the absence of something or someone that you hold near and dear. Depression is exhausting and one of the darkest stages of grief. It's like a steep mountain saturated with tears. The toughest part of climbing that mountain is the frequent slips and slides in and out of depression. It's also tough facing the reality that your reward is not what you've lost. Your reward is the strength you gain through the climb.

I recently lost a longtime friend due to disloyalty. Initially I was in denial. I then became angry and attempted to express my feelings. I thought expressing my feelings would make it better, but I eventually decided to walk away from the friendship. That led me into depression as the sorrow of losing a close friend consumed my mind daily.

Then one day I had an epiphany. I wasn't the disloyal friend that they had been but had inadvertently blamed myself for the rift. Once I had this realization, I was able to make my steady climb up the mountain of depression knowing that at the top I would still possess the characteristics of a good friend and would make more friends along the way. Suffering through this grief has taught me the wisdom of discretion. Depression is the birthing pain necessary for growth and the emergence of a newfound perspective on life.

Acceptance, the final stage of grief, seems to have no end. The memories lingering in your mind about what you have lost are hard to erase (and that's not always a bad thing). Acceptance doesn't mean you're so easily "over it". Unless you're a heartless person, you never fully get over it. Acceptance is acknowledging that what has happened has happened. Period. There's nothing you can do to reverse time and change the outcome.

Acceptance is an act of mindfulness as you strive to live in the present with each passing moment. This allows you to see your life clearly and make better decisions concerning your future. The circumstances surrounding your grief may have been horribly painful, but the strength you've gained through the process of grief will be the strength that supports the new life unfolding before you.

"Nothing brings down walls as surely as acceptance"
Deepak Chopra, The Third Jesus: The Christ We Cannot Ignore

Suffering through loss takes mental fortitude and a commitment to working through the 5 stages of grief. Using the tools and resources available to work through loss will lead you to heal and usher you into new terrains in life. It's necessary to not simply focus on the negative emotions you feel, but to find the silver lining as you fight for the growth lying ahead of you. No matter if you are grieving the loss of a loved one or a sudden career change due to termination, there's beauty that can be found as you heal.

I didn't believe that I would survive the drastic changes that I have faced recently. Initially, I fought to avoid my feelings and instead chose to remain numb. But once I embraced the circumstances around me and found the tools needed to get through the pain, I found the courage to face reality and move forward with my life. The anecdotal details I've provided transpired within a year, but working through the stages of grief with a growth mindset has helped me discover and pursue a more productive and fulfilling life.

I pray that sharing my journey has been a place of enlightenment for you. For whatever you may be facing, for whatever you have gone through - Peace be unto you.

"When you choose to prove to yourself how powerful you really are, you have no idea who you will be helping in the future."
Dr. Joe Dispenza, Becoming Supernatural: How Common People are Doing the Uncommon

For Bookings ~
Roderick Pittman
AmorFati.Bookings@outlook.com